TITANS
OF BUSINESS

STEVE JOBS

Nick Hunter

**Mishawaka-Penn-Harris
Public Library
Mishawaka, Indiana**

www.capstonepub.com
Visit our website to find out more information about Heinemann-Raintree books.

To order:
 Phone 800-747-4992
Visit www.capstonepub.com to browse our catalog and order online.

Edited by Mark Friedman, Nancy Dickmann, and Claire Throp
Designed by Richard Parker
Picture research by Liz Alexander
Original Illustrations © Capstone Global Library Ltd 2012
Illustrations by Darren Lingard

Originated by Capstone Global Library Ltd
Printed and bound in the USA by CG Book Printers

16 15 14 13 12
10 9 8 7 6 5 4 3 2 1

Library of Congress Cataloging-in-Publication Data
Hunter, Nick.
  Steve Jobs / Nick Hunter.
    p. cm.—(Titans of business)
  Includes bibliographical references and index.
  ISBN 978-1-4329-6428-3 (hb)—ISBN 978-1-4329-6435-1 (pb) 1. Jobs, Steve, 1955-2011—Juvenile literature. 2. Apple Computer, Inc.—Juvenile literature. 3. Businessmen—United States—Biography—Juvenile literature. 4. Computer engineers—United States—Biography. 5. Computer industry—United States—Juvenile literature. I. Title.
  HD9696.2.U62J6357 2013
  338.7'61004092—dc23   2011043547
  [B]

Acknowledgments
We would like to thank the following for permission to reproduce photographs: Alamy pp. 15 (© Qrt), 25 (© Pictorial Press Ltd), 33 (© Patrick Batchelder); Corbis pp. 8 (© Kimberly White), 13 (© Kim Kulish), 18 (© Bettmann), 20 (© Ed Kashi), 22 (© Ed Kashi/VII), 26 (© Christoph Dernbach/epa), 30 (© Frederic Larson/San Francisco Chronicle), 41 (© Lou Dematteis/Reuters); Getty Images pp. 9 (Jan Persson/Redferns), 10 (Bates Littlehales/National Geographic), 17 (John Chiasson), 19 (Bernard Gotfryd), 21 (Joe McNally), 37 (Brian Ach/WireImage), 39 (Justin Sullivan), 29; Mary Evans p. 11 (Interfoto/TV-yesterday); Press Association Images pp. 12, 14 (AP), 31 (John Stillwell/PA Archive), 34 (Miao Yifan/AP), 43 (Paul Sakuma/AP); Rex Features pp. 5 (KPA/Zuma), 24 (Crollalanza), 27 (Sipa Press).

Cover photographs reproduced with permission of Getty Images/Justin Sullivan (main image) and Shutterstock/© Eky Studio (background image).

Every effort has been made to contact copyright holders of any material reproduced in this book. Any omissions will be rectified in subsequent printings if notice is given to the publisher.

Contents

Find out what you need to do to have a successful career like Steve Jobs.

Read what Steve Jobs had to say or what was said about him.

Learn more about the people who influenced Steve Jobs.

Discover more about the businesses that were important during Steve Jobs's career.

Words printed in **bold** are explained in the glossary.

Who Was Steve Jobs?

Rumors had been circulating on Internet **blogs** and forums for weeks. Apple was planning a new product launch. The new product was kept very secret. Would it be a "game changer" like Apple's iPod, which changed the way people listened to music? Would it be the next "must-have" gadget following the success of the iPhone? On January 27, 2010, journalists and industry figures gathered in San Francisco, California, to listen to the man who would unveil the new device—Steve Jobs.

Apple's leader

Steve Jobs was the founder and **chief executive officer (CEO)** of Apple. He started the company with his friend Steve Wozniak in 1976, before computers had become a feature of every home and office. Jobs made Apple into one of the biggest and most admired technology companies in the world. Over the years, he came to represent his company more than almost any other business leader.

Each new Apple product is greeted with huge excitement by the **media** and the company's many fans. The iPad **tablet computer** Jobs launched in 2010 was just the latest new product to combine design and cutting-edge technology.

Reaching the top

Jobs did not become the multi-**billionaire** leader of one of the world's most admired companies by accident. His story was one of hard work, **innovation**, and making brave decisions about the future of his business, often against the advice of other people. **Entrepreneurs** need to have a fierce belief in what they are doing, but they also need to adjust when things do not go as planned.

Jobs was at the center of Apple's product announcements. In his trademark black shirt and jeans, he showed just as much enthusiasm as anyone in his audience for the stylish design and technical wizardry of Apple's products.

Childhood and Early Life

Steven Paul Jobs was born in San Francisco on February 24, 1955. He was adopted by Paul and Clara Jobs within a short time of his birth. Shortly afterward, the family moved to Mountain View, California.

Jobs's family was not wealthy. Paul Jobs had several different jobs, and times were often tough. In his spare time, Paul enjoyed fixing cars and selling them to earn extra money. Steve would sometimes accompany him to the area's scrapyards to look for old cars and parts but, according to his father, Steve "really wasn't interested in getting his hands dirty."

Education and electronics

Anyone looking to predict Jobs's huge success would have received very few clues from his early school career. Steve was intelligent, but he found it difficult to motivate himself. At the age of nine, his teacher Imogene Hill spotted this and began bribing him with a few dollars to complete his work.

"Steve is an excellent reader. However he wastes much time during reading period ... He has great difficulty motivating himself or seeing the purpose of studying reading ... He can be a discipline problem at times."

Jobs's sixth-grade report card

In later years, the area where Jobs grew up would become known as Silicon Valley, because it was home to so many technology companies. This unofficial name developed because a chemical called silicon is used to make electronic circuits.

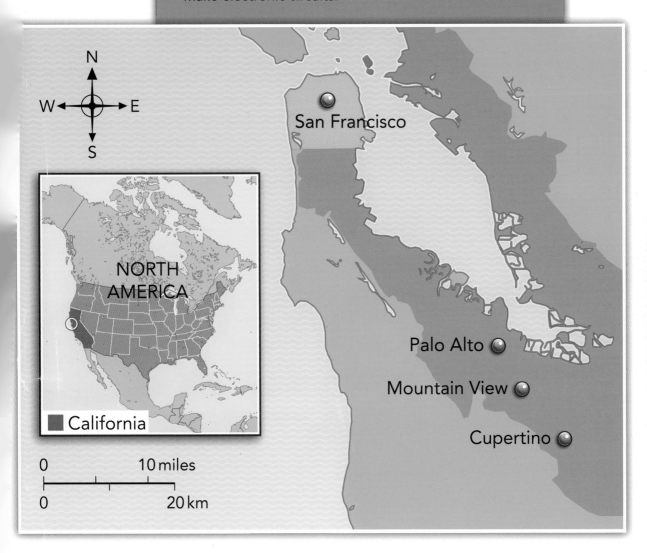

Electronics were one thing that did excite the young Jobs. One of the family's neighbors introduced him to the inner workings of microphones and televisions. This passion for electronics would develop when he moved to Cupertino's Homestead High School and started to investigate more complex electronics.

Jobs and Wozniak

Although Jobs was fascinated by electronics, he also loved literature, art, and movies. He enjoyed playing practical jokes, which often got him in trouble—like the time when he and some friends hoisted a car onto the roof of the school cafeteria.

Jobs had a reputation as a bit of a loner at school. The friends he did have were also interested in electronics. The most obsessed of all was Stephen "Woz" Wozniak, who was a few years older than Jobs and had already tried building his own computer. According to Jobs, Wozniak "was the first person I met who knew more electronics than I did."

Jobs's friendship with Steve Wozniak (left) had a powerful influence on his life and the history of personal computers.

Garage gadgets

Jobs, Wozniak, and their friends played around with electronics in their parents' garages, developing gadgets that they would show off at science fairs. Jobs and Wozniak's first **business venture** together started when Jobs was still in school. They made and sold a device called a "blue box" that could make free phone calls. Wozniak made the boxes, and Jobs urged him to turn it into a business. The result was a success—but it was also against the law, and so it did not last long.

In addition to a shared passion for electronics, Jobs and Wozniak also loved the music of Bob Dylan.

Risking failure

Jobs's heroes did not come from the world of business. One of them, Bob Dylan, was a singer-songwriter who changed popular music forever. Another was Pablo Picasso, one of the world's greatest artists. Jobs later said that he learned a lot from these heroes because they were always trying new things and "always risking failure."

An independent mind

As soon as he could drive, Jobs used his battered red Fiat to visit friends at colleges near his home. This gave him a taste of independence. After graduating from high school, he decided to attend Reed College in Portland, Oregon, rather than any of the colleges near his home.

Jobs was always an independent thinker. He found that studying at Reed did not suit him, and he soon dropped out. However, he still sometimes went to classes that interested him, such as **calligraphy**. His time at college gave him the chance to pursue many different ideas. He became a vegetarian and studied the religion of **Zen Buddhism**, which would have a major influence in his later life.

Jobs's decision to go to Reed College gave him the chance to explore the mountains and coastline around Portland, Oregon.

In 1974, Jobs left Reed College for good without graduating. He returned to California and got a job designing arcade games for Atari, one of the world's first video game companies. While working at Atari, he met up again with Steve Wozniak.

Pong was very basic by today's standards, but it was very popular.

Atari

Atari was founded by Nolan Bushnell. In 1972, it produced Pong, one of the first arcade games. The company went on to produce the Atari Games Console for playing at home, through the user's television. Like many companies in Silicon Valley, Atari was started by young entrepreneurs with very little business experience but some good ideas. Businesses like Atari deliberately tried to be different from more traditional companies.

Apple Computer

The mid-1970s were interesting times for computer **hobbyists**. In 1975, Jobs and Wozniak became excited by the Altair 8800, one of the first personal computers. The Altair's key part was a **microprocessor** chip, which meant computers could be small enough to sit on a desk. Before that, computers were only found in large companies and government offices, and a single computer could fill a whole room.

Apple's core

Wozniak used the microprocessor to design his own computer. He was then working for the computer company Hewlett-Packard, but the company was not interested in developing his product. Jobs persuaded Wozniak that they could sell the **circuit board** used in the computer and make some money.

Computers like the Altair 8800 were not designed to appeal to the general user.

Jobs suggested the name Apple for their new business venture, perhaps because it reminded him of when he worked in an apple orchard as a student. To finance the new business, Jobs sold his Volkswagen van and Wozniak sold his programmable calculator, a valuable item in 1976. Both men were still only in their twenties.

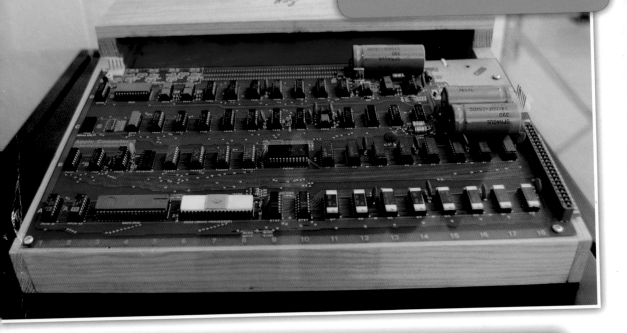

The Apple I circuit board was a long way from the stylish gadgets that Apple is known for today.

Steve Wozniak (born 1950)

Apple Computer could not have existed without the technical and engineering genius of Wozniak. Wozniak always saw himself as an engineer, and he left the business side of the Apple project to Jobs. He has said that he came along at just the right time, when computers were small and simple enough that one person could design and build one. After being seriously injured in a plane crash in 1981, Wozniak left Apple in 1985 to complete his studies and pursue projects in education.

A computer for everyone

The Apple I circuit board was assembled in Jobs's parents' garage. It was popular with hobbyists, who combined it with monitors and other parts to make their own computers. However, Jobs had bigger ambitions for Apple. Wozniak was the technical wizard, but Jobs's skill lay in predicting what customers wanted. He saw a market for a complete personal computer— but it would have to look right.

A new kind of Apple

The Apple II was presented to the public in 1977. Its attractive plastic case made it look very different from the computers that had come before it. At that time, Jobs's idea of putting a computer in a molded plastic box was completely new. He took his inspiration for styles and colors by looking at kitchen appliances in a local department store. However, the Apple II's color display, keyboard, and other features created by Wozniak were a key factor in making the Apple II the fastest-selling personal computer in history at that time.

Jobs said that he got the idea for the Apple II's plastic case from a food processor.

The success of the Apple II made Apple into a multi-million-dollar business. But the company was still run by Jobs and Wozniak—two young, long-haired guys who built computers in garages. Could they take their business to the next level?

Apple's **logo** is one of the best-known symbols in business, although it does not include the company name. The bite was added so people would know it was an apple and not a tomato.

"It was clear to me that for every **hardware** hobbyist who wanted to assemble his own computer, there were a thousand people who ... wanted to mess around with **programming** ... just like I did when I was 10."

Jobs on the Apple II

Building the business

Despite Apple's early success, it was only one of hundreds of technology companies in the area of California known as Silicon Valley. Many of these companies were replaced or merged with others over the years. Some, such as Hewlett-Packard and Sun Microsystems, achieved lasting success.

The search was on to find **investors** and experienced people to help Apple grow. Jobs, with his long hair, jeans, and sandals, did not always make a good impression. One potential investor said that Jobs "looked like a renegade from the human race." Despite this, Apple was able to find the investment and advice it needed.

New people joining the company also meant that Jobs and Wozniak did not always get their own way. This often caused tensions, as Jobs's passion and energy clashed with the rules and processes introduced by people like Michael Scott, Apple's CEO from 1977 to 1981.

Raising money

Many ideas, especially in technology, are funded at their earliest stages by venture capital or "angel investors." Venture capital funds can provide money for entrepreneurs to develop their ideas. Venture capitalists must take extraordinary risks—but they can also get high rewards. "Angel investors" are usually rich and can afford to fund new businesses. Later on, banks lend money that has to be repaid with an added amount called interest. Investors buy shares in the company in return for a proportion of the company's future profits. To persuade people to invest, entrepreneurs need to have a convincing plan of how their business will make money.

Going public

Despite these growing pains, business was booming. In 1980, **shares** in Apple Computer Inc. were offered to the public. Apple's launch was the biggest since the Ford Motor Company, and it made Jobs an estimated $250 million overnight. However, Jobs was not always comfortable with his newfound wealth. "You run out of things to buy real quick," he said.

The stock market is where shares in businesses are bought and sold.

Point and click

Although the Apple II was a step forward, personal computers were still very complicated to use for most people. Rather than using a mouse to point and click, users had to type commands. Computer screens showed lines of text rather than the desktop and windows that were developed later.

During a visit to the Xerox Corporation's research center, Jobs saw something that would change the way people used computers. The **graphical user interface (GUI)** was laid out like a desktop with overlapping pages. Users pointed and clicked a mouse to open programs. Jobs thought Apple could improve on this GUI and set his engineers to work.

Jobs (left) stands at a computer conference with CEO John Sculley (center; see page 20) and Steve Wozniak. Jobs's presentations to the media made him the public face of Apple.

Commitment to quality

Jobs had a reputation as a tough man to work for. He was totally focused on making Apple's products as good as they possibly could be. If this meant endless redesigning, Jobs demanded it. While these demands were sometimes difficult to deal with, they also inspired the people who worked with him.

The "insanely great" Macintosh

The GUI became a key part of Jobs's next project—the Apple Macintosh, or Mac. He assembled a small team of the best people he could find. The Mac would be more than just great— it would be "insanely great."

Jobs insisted that the designers of the Mac produce several different versions until he was happy. It is said that Jobs even ordered an internal circuit board to be redesigned because he did not like the look of it. The Macintosh was launched in January 1984, but by that time there were signs of change in the world of personal computers.

The Mac's monitor sat on top of the computer, with no messy wires between the two.

PC problems

The Macintosh certainly looked great, but it was not an immediate success. The first models were not powerful enough to run users' **software**, and there was a limited amount of software available. Apple also faced tough competition from the computer giant IBM. Whereas Apple developed its own hardware and software, other computer makers used software made by Microsoft.

Apple crumbles

It became clear that Apple needed an experienced businessperson to lead the company. Some people even said that Jobs needed "adult supervision." In 1983, John Sculley, a former **executive** with the soft drink company Pepsi, was chosen by Jobs to be Apple's new CEO.

John Sculley (right) found that working with Jobs at Apple was very different from his experience in the soft drink industry.

At first Sculley and Jobs worked well together, but problems soon began to surface. Jobs liked and expected to be in control, but Sculley was not prepared to allow that. In 1985, Sculley convinced Apple's board of directors that the company would be more successful without Jobs. Jobs left the company he had founded.

Could the company prosper without its **chairperson** and founder? And what would Jobs do now?

"Do you want to sell sugar water all your life or do you want to change the world?"

Jobs tries to persuade Pepsi's John Sculley to join Apple

Like Jobs, Bill Gates founded his company in the 1970s. When Jobs was forced to leave Apple in 1985, Gates was able to guide Microsoft to dominate the world of software.

Microsoft

The world's biggest software company was started by Bill Gates and Paul Allen in 1976. In 1980, Microsoft developed the **operating system** for IBM's personal computer. The Windows GUI followed. It adopted many of the features of Apple's GUI and became the standard software for most business and personal computers around the world. Microsoft was generally seen as less innovative than Apple, but its success came because its products worked with many different companies' computers.

NeXT Steps

In 1985, Jobs was still only 30 years old. He had achieved more in his nine years with Apple than most businesspeople manage in a lifetime. He had enough money that he never needed to work again—but that was not Jobs's style. He still had something to prove, and he wanted revenge for the way Apple had treated him.

The black cube of the NeXT computer did have one huge effect on the history of technology. Tim Berners-Lee was using a NeXT computer when he developed the system of organizing information on the Internet using **hypertext**. This formed the foundation of the World Wide Web.

22

What's NeXT?

Jobs's next venture was to provide computers for schools. The birth of the NeXT Corporation was a big contrast to the early days of Apple. The company had millions of dollars in financial backing and a logo created by a top designer. The lavish offices could not have been more different from Apple's first home in the Jobs's family garage.

NeXT was a rare lesson in failure for Jobs. He had misjudged his potential customers in schools and colleges, who were happy to stick with companies they knew rather than Jobs's stylish new computer. In 1993, Jobs decided that NeXT should concentrate on selling software. Many wondered whether this would be the end of his starring role in the computer revolution.

Find out what you are good at

All entrepreneurs need to recognize the things they are good at. All Jobs's success had been built on the simple idea that computers could be made attractive and accessible to individual customers. People who bought computers for large businesses or schools were much less interested in the great design and simplicity that defined Jobs's most successful products. It is important to know when you need outside help, as Jobs learned by the time he got involved in the movie industry (see pages 24 and 25).

Making movies

In 1986, Jobs bought a computer animation studio called the Graphics Group from movie director George Lucas. Jobs would later rename it Pixar. He was mainly interested in Pixar because he wanted to create computer animation software. However, beginning with *Toy Story* in 1995, the studio created some of the most successful animated films of all time.

Pixar was a great example of Jobs's belief in building a team of the best people. At Apple, he had a reputation for interfering in all aspects of a project. But Jobs knew that he could not do the same when it came to film animation. Pixar used the same team to make all its movies, which is unusual in Hollywood. Jobs trusted his team to deliver, and he was not disappointed. In 2006, Pixar was sold to Disney for $74 billion.

George Lucas became famous as the director of the *Star Wars* movies. His company also **pioneered** new techniques for computer-generated special effects.

Toy Story was the first fully computer-animated feature film.

Pixar

When Jobs bought Pixar, it focused on developing computer animation software and working with companies such as Disney. John Lasseter was the animator at the heart of Pixar's success. In 1995, he directed *Toy Story*. He worked on many of the successes that followed, including sequels to *Toy Story*, *Finding Nemo* (2003), *The Incredibles* (2004), and *Up* (2009).

Rotten Apple

Meanwhile, Apple had not done well without its founder. The Mac had become popular with a minority of customers and creative businesses, but most homes and offices were buying personal computers running Microsoft software. Apple's power to innovate and excite customers seemed to have left along with Jobs and Wozniak. By the mid-1990s, it looked as if Apple might disappear altogether.

Back on Board

In 1996, Apple was in trouble. The company had not created a new hit product since the Apple Mac, and it was struggling to replace its aging software. Apple decided to solve this software problem by buying NeXT-step. This was the remainder of Jobs's NeXT company. As part of the deal, Apple also started working with its founder once more.

Shortly afterward, Apple's board asked Jobs to lead the company again. CEO John Sculley had left in 1993, and his successors had been unable to help Apple regain its reputation for innovation. However, few people believed that Jobs could revive Apple. He had been out of the limelight for more than 10 years, while former rivals such as Microsoft's Bill Gates had come to dominate the world of technology.

Apple's offices in Cupertino, California, are just a short distance from where Jobs grew up.

Tough decisions

Jobs's success had always come from making great computers that people could use with ease. He knew that if he was going to rescue Apple, he needed to make some tough decisions. So he canceled many Apple projects that did not meet his high standards.

It was one thing to put an end to projects and identify what was wrong. But so much had changed since Jobs left Apple, and the company was now working in a fast-moving industry. For example, in 1985 the Internet did not even exist for general use. Now there was a computer on everyone's desk. Did people still want what Jobs and Apple had to offer?

"Apple has some tremendous **assets** but I believe without some attention, the company could, could, could—I'm searching for the right word—could, could die."

Jobs, talking to *Time* magazine in 1997

Keep it simple

The first visible result of Jobs's return to Apple was a computer that looked unlike any other. The iMac, launched in 1998, combined screen and computer inside a colored case. It was **marketed** as a simple way to access the Internet—a new experience for many people at that time.

One of the features of Jobs's products was what was left out. He always aimed to make his products as clean and simple as possible, so as to limit the amount of choices the user has to make. For example, the iMac had no **floppy disk** drive. Jobs correctly predicted that the floppy disk was dying out, to be replaced by CD and online transfer of data.

The iMac quickly became one of the most popular computers of all time. However, it was not perfect. Jobs admitted that he "felt like a dope" for not including a CD burner as part of the early iMacs. Rival companies benefited from this mistake, causing iMac sales to decline by 2000.

Continuing the revival

Despite the success of Apple's new products, there was still a long way to go to revive the company. Growing use of the Internet was changing many areas of business. For his next trick, Jobs planned to take on another industry altogether.

Innovation

The best entrepreneurs succeed because they do something that other people have not thought of yet. Jobs's greatest successes came from doing something new or doing something in a new way. Partly, this innovation came because Jobs was naturally creative and curious about the world. He also encouraged innovation among the people he worked with.

"In terms of an inspirational leader, Steve Jobs is really the best I've ever met."

Bill Gates of Microsoft, speaking in 1998

At a time when most computers were produced in very dull colors, the iMac stood out from the crowd.

Digital music

As Internet use took off in the late 1990s, sharing and listening to music online became enormously popular. Jobs admits that he was a bit slow in understanding the huge changes in digital music. He decided that Apple had to get involved—but there was some catching up to do. The first step was Apple's iTunes, launched in January 2001. This was software that helped users organize their music.

There were already MP3 players available in 2001, but they were complex to use and could not hold much more music than a CD. Jobs was confident that Apple could improve on them. Once again, a small team worked on the project that would become the iPod.

Birth of the iPod

The first iPod was launched in October 2001, and it was described by Jobs as a "major, major breakthrough." Sales were steady, with 600,000 iPods sold by the end of 2002. In 2003, the online iTunes store began to sell digital music downloads. Customers discovered that they could carry a whole music collection on a gadget no bigger than a deck of cards. By 2011, around 300 million iPods had been sold.

Jobs boasted that the first iPod would give users "1,000 songs in your pocket." Apple continually refined the iPod, launching color and touch-screen versions that could hold thousands of songs as well as other media such as video.

The success of the iPod and iTunes also changed the way people bought music. People began to download their music rather than buying CDs. Apple had changed the music industry forever.

Jonathan Ive (born 1967)

British-born Ive is the modest design **guru** behind many of Apple's most stylish products. He stresses the importance of teamwork in developing their designs. He says that their work is about solving complex problems so the solutions "appear ... incredibly simple, so you have no sense how difficult this thing was."

More Than Computers

With the launch of the iPod in 2001, Apple became more than just a computer company. It was now competing against companies that made mass-market products such as televisions and DVD players. Jobs's return to Apple was looking like one of the most inspired moves in the history of business.

Apple had always been unusual in that it produced both hardware and software. Rivals such as Microsoft concentrated only on software. With iTunes, Apple now provided a service as well. Customers bought their music from Apple and played it on an Apple device.

Customer service was very important to Jobs. When he rejoined Apple, Jobs was unhappy with the way Apple's products were being sold by other retailers. He wanted Apple customers to have "the best buying experience." Apple Stores have become one of the fastest-growing retail chains in history. Customers love innovations such as the Genius Bar, where experienced experts can advise customers on how to get the best from Apple products.

Sony

Perhaps the closest business model for Apple has been the Japanese electronics giant Sony. Sony was also led by an innovative leader, Akio Morita, who drove the development of products such as the Walkman. The Walkman was the dominant portable music player before the arrival of MP3 players. Sony remains a huge electronics company, but it has not been able to match Apple's **iconic** products in the 2000s.

Digital hub

The expert advice at Apple Stores also gave a boost to sales of Apple computers. Jobs saw desktop or laptop computers as the "digital hub" that linked together mobile products such as the iPod.

The first Apple Store opened in 2001. This is Apple's flagship store in New York City.

Apple's consistently great products have inspired customer loyalty.

"Apple is engaged in probably the most remarkable second act ever seen in technology."

Eric Schmidt of Google, speaking to *Time* magazine

Inventing the future

Jobs and Apple continued to amaze customers and business observers. Apple's next venture into new territory was the iPhone. Calling it a "phone" told only part of the story—it was actually more like a mini-computer. Apple also encouraged software developers to create **applications**, or "apps," for the iPhone. The huge range of brilliant or bizarre apps helped to make the iPhone into Apple's most successful product.

The iPhone's combination of cell phone and computer, as well as Jobs's magic touch with design and simplicity, changed the way people thought about their phones. Established cell phone companies such as Nokia struggled to compete. Technology companies such as Google followed Apple with their own **smartphone** products.

In 2010, Apple followed the iPhone with the iPad, a computer with no keyboard, mouse, or external wires. Two million iPads were sold within two months of the tablet computer's launch. Some people predicted it would replace books and newspapers in the same way that the iPod had replaced music CDs.

Build the brand

Every Apple product, advertisement, or store is designed to build the Apple **brand**. This is the personality that the company has developed. Customers know that everything Apple does will be innovative and stylish. This meant that Apple did not have to advertise the iPhone before its release. Because it was an Apple product, customers knew it would do something new and exciting. Jobs was at the heart of those eagerly awaited product launches. The enthusiasm he had for new technology and the desire he had to make Apple's products as good as they could be were part of what made the brand so successful.

What Was Steve Jobs Really Like?

During his many years at the top of one of the world's most-watched companies, Jobs became a business legend. He was well known for his restless creativity, his attention to detail, and, sometimes, his fierce temper. Jobs's rare public appearances were often to present new Apple products, where fans hung on his every word. What was Jobs like away from the limelight?

Family life

Jobs's success made him very wealthy, but he did not live the typical billionaire lifestyle. The Jobs family lived quietly in Palo Alto, California. Steve married Laurene Powell in 1991, and the couple had three children together. Jobs also had another daughter, Lisa, from an earlier relationship.

Many of Jobs's ideas and interests changed little from the early 1970s. His fascination with Buddhism set him apart from typical business leaders, even in the informal world of Silicon Valley. He was also a passionate music fan.

Working with Jobs

Jobs had a reputation for being difficult to work with. He was passionate about Apple's success, and this often showed itself as fierce criticism of coworkers when things went wrong. However, Jobs's quest for perfection and the success he brought to Apple inspired great loyalty.

"What I learned about Steve was that he was a **visionary** who was able to motivate people to want to follow him and build great products."

John Sculley, former CEO of Apple

> "Like many people, I tried to avoid [Jobs] as much as possible. You want to ... avoid him getting mad at you."
>
> A former Apple employee

Laurene Powell Jobs is a strong supporter of educational charities.

Health problems and resignation

Jobs's successful return to Apple was overshadowed by concerns about his health. In 2004, he underwent major surgery for a rare form of cancer, and he was unable to work for several months afterward. A few years later, it emerged that the disease had returned. In 2009, Jobs had to undergo an emergency liver **transplant**.

In January 2011, he announced once again that he would be taking time off from Apple to focus on his health. On August 24, 2011, Jobs finally resigned from the company he founded. Then, on October 5, 2011, the announcement came that Jobs had died from his illness.

Business impact

The sad news of Jobs's death shocked his admirers and supporters worldwide—both in the business community and among loyal Apple customers. It also raised questions about the future of Apple. Many people who remember what happened to the company in the 1990s wonder whether it can survive without its leader. More than any other technology company, Apple's fortunes have always been closely linked to the vision of its founder.

Tim Cook (born 1960)

Tim Cook took over from Jobs during Jobs's medical leave. Cook joined the company in 1998. Before stepping into Jobs's shoes, he was responsible for the production and delivery of the products that Jobs and his creative team developed.

"With Jobs there was a guy at the beginning and end of every project who had the authority to say, 'This sucks. Start over.' Whoever replaces him may share his vision and job title, but he or she will not be the co-founder of Apple and won't have the same authority."

Philip Elmer-Dewitt, blogger on Apple, quoted in *The Times* newspaper, 2009

Jobs was clearly ill at his last public appearance in June 2011.

Assessing Steve Jobs

Jobs had a starring role in the birth of the personal computer. He then helped Pixar to become one of the greatest success stories of modern movies. From 1997 to 2011, he revived Apple, while brilliant products produced by his company revolutionized other industries such as music and telecommunications. The vision and passion of Jobs were the threads running through all these successes.

Standing alone

Many of Jobs's rivals had one great idea that brought them success, such as Mark Zuckerberg's Facebook. Jobs is the only person to have triumphed in so many different areas of technology. His genius for creative innovation together with his business skills have brought us products that range from personal computers to music, cell phones, and movies.

Visionary leader

When cancer finally claimed Jobs's life on October 5, 2011, he was mourned by both his fans and his business rivals. Tributes poured in to the "visionary" whose products and ideas changed the way millions of people worked, played, and communicated.

Be a perfectionist

There are many stories of Jobs's perfectionism—from the look of the buttons on a new piece of software to the lighting at a product launch. Apple's customers know that every detail on a new product has been discussed and probably redesigned many times. This perfectionism is what makes Apple's products stand out from the crowd.

> "Steve was among the greatest of American innovators— brave enough to think differently, bold enough to believe he could change the world, and talented enough to do it ... And there may be no greater tribute to Steve's success than the fact that much of the world learned of his passing on a device he invented."
>
> U.S. President Barack Obama pays tribute, 2011

Jobs was incredibly important to Apple. It remains to be seen how the company will do without its inspirational leader.

How to Be an Entrepreneur

From a young age, Jobs thought differently from many of the people around him. Jobs's love of electronics was a key factor in his early ideas and success. What are the things that make successful entrepreneurs, and what can they learn from Jobs's career?

Having the idea
All entrepreneurs need to have at least one good idea that sets them apart from existing businesses. Jobs believed that people wanted to buy complete, easy-to-use computers such as the Apple II.

Take a chance
Entrepreneurs have to take risks. Jobs and Wozniak took a risk when they started their own company, rather than taking their idea to someone else.

Keep going!
Another of history's great entrepreneurs, Thomas Edison, said: "Genius is 1 percent inspiration, 99 percent perspiration," meaning that there is always a lot of hard work needed before people will believe in your great new idea.

"You've got to have an idea, or a problem or a wrong that you want to right that you're passionate about otherwise you're not going to have the **perseverance** to stick it through."
Steve Jobs's advice for entrepreneurs

Know your strengths

Jobs knew that he could not do everything. Apple's first products depended on Wozniak's engineering skills. Figure out what your strengths are and find the best people to do the things you are not as good at.

Keep the ideas coming

Jobs's greatest success was his ability to turn his basic idea of making technology simple and attractive into many different products. Jobs had enough money to stop working in the 1980s, but he was always driven forward by the next product idea.

Glossary

application computer program designed to do a particular job, such as an e-mail application that is designed to send e-mails

asset something that has value

billionaire someone who is estimated to be worth more than one billion dollars, or one billion of another currency

blog short for "weblog," a series of online articles that may take the form of a journal or discussion of developments in a particular area of interest, such as technology

brand logo, name, and features of a business that make it special and make people recognize it

business venture company set up by an individual or group

calligraphy art of decorative lettering

chairperson person who leads the board that manages a company, usually working closely with the chief executive officer

chief executive officer (CEO) leading manager responsible for running a business or organization

circuit board rigid board that contains an electronic circuit

entrepreneur person who takes financial risks to set up and run new businesses

executive someone who has a senior or important job within a company

floppy disk removable disk on which users can store or transfer computer data. Floppy disks have largely been replaced by other forms of digital storage.

graphical user interface (GUI) part of a computer operating system that is designed to look like a desktop and enables users to easily access programs and documents

guru religious leader or teacher; the term has also come to mean any influential leader

hardware parts of a computer such as the electronic components, monitor, and keyboard

hobbyist someone who is interested in a particular pastime or leisure activity, such as people who are very interested in computers

hypertext software system that allows text and images to be organized and cross-referenced on web sites

iconic image or object that is extremely well known or admired

innovation new way of doing or making something

investor person who gives money to a business in order to make a profit

logo symbol or image that a company uses as its special sign

market promote and sell products

media means by which the majority of people get news or information; it includes television, newspapers, Internet, and radio

microprocessor integrated electronic circuit that is the central processing unit of a personal computer

operating system software that manages the functions of a computer

perseverance ability to continue with a task in spite of difficulties

pioneer lead the way for others to follow

programming creating programs for use with computers

share part of the value of a company, which can be bought

smartphone phone that is more like a mini-computer with web browsing, e-mail, and other applications

software programs used by a computer to perform tasks

tablet computer computer in which a touch screen replaces additional parts like a keyboard and mouse

transplant operation to replace a damaged body part or organ with a healthy one

visionary someone with a clear vision of how to achieve something or make a business successful

Zen Buddhism form of the religion of Buddhism that emphasizes the importance of meditation

Find Out More

Books

Deane-Pratt, Ade. *Electrical Gadgets* (How Things Work). New York: PowerKids, 2012.

Gillam, Scott. *Steve Jobs: Apple & iPod Wizard* (Essential Lives). Edina, Minn.: ABDO, 2008.

Goldsmith, Mike, et al. *Computer* (Eyewitness). New York: Dorling Kindersley, 2011.

Imbimbo, Anthony. *Steve Jobs: The Brilliant Mind Behind Apple* (Life Portraits). Pleasantville, N.Y.: Gareth Stevens, 2009.

Oxlade, Chris. *The Computer* (Tales of Invention). Chicago: Heinemann Library, 2011.

Sutherland, Adam. *The Story of Apple* (The Business of High Tech). New York: Rosen Central, 2012.

Web sites

www.allaboutstevejobs.com

This web site includes information and videos about the Apple founder.

www.apple.com/pr/products/ipodhistory

You can find lots of information on the official Apple web site. This timeline charts the history of the iPod and iTunes.

www.pixar.com/companyinfo/history/index.html

Learn more about the history of Pixar on the company's own web site.

www.ted.com/talks/steve_jobs_how_to_live_before_you_die.html

This is a video of a speech that Jobs made at Stanford University, in California, covering topics such as the importance of calligraphy and what he learned when he was fired by the company he started.

www.theapplemuseum.com

Find out about the history of Apple on this web site. It includes lots of pictures of Apple products from the past.

Topics to research

After reading this book, which details about Jobs most interest you? What business ideas can you think of after reading about his success? To learn more, you might want to research the following topics:

- The history of the personal computer: Find out about the developments in technology that led to the connected world we live in today.
- Digital music: Discover how the iPod and online music changed the music industry.
- Pioneers: Find out more about the lives of some of the technology pioneers mentioned in this book. Who created your favorite gadget or web application? Why was this person successful?

You can visit your local library to learn more about any of these fascinating subjects.

Index